Book of Anonymous Letters™

Amelia Anhalt and Kaitlyn Conmy

Dedicated To: All the letters never sent

You may be reading what was written to you

First, we want to thank everyone who submitted a letter.

When we created this project, we had no idea how many people we would reach.

One night, we were on the phone with each other talking about how cool it would be to write a book. We were bouncing ideas off of one another until we came up with one we both really liked.

"We should create a book full of anonymous letters from people all over the world!"

We stayed on the phone, and that night made a website where people could submit anonymous letters. We left instructions vague so that people could write whatever they wanted. That night, we posted a Tik Tok about it, not expecting much.

When we woke up the next morning, it had gone viral. Within weeks, over 3 million people had seen our video, and so many of them wanted to write.

We had no idea the outpouring of emotion this idea would fuel. We never expected so many people to embrace the idea and find in this effort a safe place to share, vent, reveal and rage. Grateful does not even begin to describe how we feel. This is not just our book anymore. It is your book, it is everyone's book. Regardless of whether your letter is in the book, thank you. Thank you for writing a letter. Thank you for being vulnerable. And thank you for sharing your story.

TRIGGER WARNING

Many of these letters include stories about triggering topics, like sexual assault, abuse, rape, suicide, self-harm, depression, and eating disorders, among others. Please read with caution. We do not want these letters to traumatize anyone. When we launched the website, we did not realize that so many letters would be full of topics like these. However, we felt that we should include them because they expose lots of hardship and injustice in the world. People who have endured or are going through these things need to be heard.

We all need to be heard.

CONTENT WARNING

This book contains explicit language which may be offensive to some readers.

If the topics are triggering, or the language and/or content offensive, please do not read.

Resources

If you or anyone you know is struggling with any of the topics covered in these letters, including self-harm, suicidal thoughts, an eating disorder, depression, sexual assault, and domestic violence; please seek help. There are a lot of free resources out there and most states also have specialized free resources available, but here is a short list of nationwide help sites that we found once we realized how many people who wrote letters might need this:

You deserve happiness, safety, and a long life.

National Suicide Prevention Lifeline: 800-273-8255

National Domestic Violence Hotline: www.thehotline.org

Crisis Text Line: https://www.crisistextline.org/

National Eating Disorders Association: https://www.nationaleatingdisorders.org/help-support/contact-helpline

Because there were over 500,000 submissions, we could only include a fraction of the submissions.

Follow us on Tik Tok and Instagram (@bookofanonymousletters)

You can always submit a letter on our website
(www.bookofanonymousletters.weebly.com).
Contact us at (contactbookofanonymousletters@gmail.com)

Note: Our intention was to publish the letters as they came to us; however, some editorial changes have been made to certain letters so that last names are not disclosed and minor typographical and formatting changes have been made for purposes of presentation.

To: The Reader

Enjoy the little things
The feeling of being at the airport and hugging the one you
haven't seen in forever.
The late-night drives blasting music with your friends.
The feeling right before you kiss them.
The first drop in a roller coaster.
The view of the stars when you're camping.
The feeling when they remember a small detail from forever ago.
The dogs with their heads out the window.
The beautiful sunsets and sunrises that mark a new beginning.
The "This made me think of you."
The feeling of blowing out your birthday candles.
The smell of the rain.
The perfect ratio of frosting to a cupcake.
The last-minute decisions.
The singing at the top of your lungs.
The time you first hear a really good song.
The perfect vanilla latte.
The butterflies in your stomach.
The last day of school before summer vacation.
The feeling when you can't stop laughing.
Enjoy them. Enjoy them all. Because I just learned to. And it's
awesome.

To: Alex

Just friends. I can be friends. So maybe my heart skips a beat when I get a text from you. But that's okay because we're friends now. Friends who talk about anything. And we talk about this guy you've been talking to. The guy who's honestly an asshole. Do you even know what he does when you're not around? But I haven't seen you this happy in a long time. So I'm happy for you. We talk about this girl in my math class. The one that's always smiling at me. I tell you about the little doodles she always passes to me and you tell me to ask her out. But I don't. I make excuses, and I tell you I don't think she likes me or she's just being friendly. I tell you she's not my type. I don't tell you that no one is my type, or that I look for you in everyone I talk to. Not because I'm not over you, although I'm not, but because you're perfect.
Because when I say I look for you, I mean I look for that face you make when you're bored. I mean I look for the way your nose scrunches when you're trying not to laugh. I look for the way you bring energy into everything you do. I look for the way you make me want to be a better person, for you. I look for you in everyone I meet, but I find you in none.
I had you, and then I lost you, and now we're friends. And I'm okay with being friends. Even if every time we make eye contact my heart aches and I can see a little sadness in your eyes. And it takes everything out of me to not beg you. I want a second chance, a chance to make things right. A chance to do everything I didn't the first time, to give you what you deserve. But I don't say anything because I don't deserve a second chance. Because I had you, and then lost you. And now we're just friends.

To: My Pets In Heaven (Or Wherever There Is An Afterlife)

I hope you know how much I love you, and how much I wish I could take back all the times I said "no" and "stop it." If only I could make you feel safe and loved one last time, I would, I hope you know.

To: K

I would give you all of my blue jolly ranchers<3

To: That One Teacher

Thank you for saving my life, having hope in me, and believing in me when no one else did. Thank you for letting me rant to you about my trashy life and thank you for being you. Thank you.

To: Mom

First, I want you to know that I love you and I look up to you in a lot of ways. You are so strong. You have helped my older sister and me get through high school and into college, and you're raising our little sister by yourself. I am very proud of you. As much as I love you, I know your love for me is probably conditional. From the conversations we have had, the way I have seen you react to others, and the way you raised me, I know that you don't believe people should love others of the same gender. You have trouble believing that people can exist outside of the gender binary. I know you would not be fully accepting if I came out to you. That hurts. However, I do know that people are capable of change. I believe that you are capable of changing your views. When the day arrives that I come out to you, I hope and pray you will love, support, and accept me. That you will be there for me, as well as my future significant other. Until that day, I am praying for you. You are my mom and I love you.

To: The Girl That Died:

This is my story; I hope it continues yours. On May 8th, 2019 I almost took my life. I was alone in my darkroom with pills in one hand and a glass of water in the other. I was in tears crying with all of these emotions and thoughts rushing through me, though it felt so numb at the same time. I was so close to ending this story of mine. As if nothing had mattered at all, not even the consequences of my death. I was determined with my decision. I had considered it for months, and it felt like I couldn't take it much longer until I had something close to a vision. A vision of myself living in moments of what my future life had in store for me. I was smiling in all of these moments. It was as if I could feel how I would exactly feel in these sort of future memories. The feeling was happy. I could see myself happy for the first time in a long time. Though they were only moments, I knew it was enough. Those moments of my future life where I find myself infinitely happy are worth staying. Continuing this story of mine. No one saved me, it was me who saved myself. My future story kept me here. So I made a promise to my future self that I would never consider something like ending my story ever again. Something died in me that night. The girl who wanted to give up died that night. So anytime I live one of those happy moments I envision, I write to her to tell her how much she's missed out on. I make her feel guilty for the way she felt. I use a colon to represent my story. "to the girl that died: you had your first kiss" "to the girl that died: you met your first love" "to the girl that died: that boy asked you out on your first date" "to the girl that died: you found your soulmate in your best friend" "to the girl that died: you danced in the rain with the girl you love" "to the girl that died: you learned to love and accept who you are" There are many more journal entries to come and many more happy moments I'll get to tell her about, but for now to the girl that died: you made it. Thank you for staying.

To: Dad

Dad, I wish you hadn't died. I wish you were still here. I wish you could have seen me graduate high school. I wish you were there for my eighteenth birthday. I wish you could move me into college. I wish you could help me navigate my future. I wish you could see the person I am now. I wish I knew if you were proud of me. I wish I could hear you tell me you loved me. I wish we could go on one more drive in your truck and listen to country music. I wish you could take me to one more baseball game. I wish I could watch you brew beer again. I wish I could help you make pancakes on a Sunday night. I wish I could buy you the next book from your favorite author. I wish you were there to help me with my car. I wish I didn't have to navigate life knowing I won't see you again. I wish I could give you one more hug. I wish I could tell you I love you. I wish I could tell you that you were an amazing dad. I wish you were here.

To: Ko

A few weeks ago when we were laying in your bed, you told me
you loved me. I didn't react because it was so unexpected. You
told me you couldn't kiss me. I know it is because of your girl in
Paris and the promise you made to her, but still, I'm frustrated. I
guess it's because I love you too. It's been four years since we
met, and I've loved you ever since. As I told you on that day we
were laying on your bed, I truly don't want things to get serious
again between us. We both know it wouldn't make sense for
now. But I realized that I'd still like to be the only person you
love, and I want to kiss you so bad. I obviously don't want to
mess up what you have with that girl because I can see how
much she seems to matter to you. I don't expect you to end your
relationship with her just for us to kiss once, also because I still
like our friendship. But just know that I love you, and I'll be here,
in Lyon, waiting for us to find each other again, as we have been
doing for the past few years. Take care, I hope I'll see you again
soon.

To: **Whoever** Needs A Reason To Stay

When I was 13 years old I tried to kill myself. I wanted to die so **badly** that I walked into traffic. No harm was done physically, but mentally I fucked myself up. At such a young age, I was in such a horrible place that I didn't want to live anymore. There was nothing worth living for. Or so I thought. I'm now 19 years old, a sophomore in college, and happier than ever with where I am in life. Yes, it could be better. The impending doom of crippling student debt is not a fun concept, but that's life. I am the first of my siblings to go to college, and I have sure made my parents proud.

And you might be asking yourself "but Anon, my parents could never be proud of me." Well, guess what, I may not be your parent but I'm sure as hell proud of you.

I'm proud that you are awake right now. I'm proud that you are alive. I'm proud of all your accomplishments, no matter how big or small. If you ate today, I'm proud. If you tried and couldn't eat it's okay. I'm still proud of you because you're staying strong. You're tough, you're a fighter.

You wanna know why? Because you're reading this. I know you probably don't want to hear the sappy bullshit about how people will miss you, because yeah they will. But what about all the **things you'll miss? There** are so many things in the world that **you have yet to discover**: new foods, new places, new music, **new books, new** movies, etc. There are so many sunsets and **sunrises to** see. There are dogs or cats to pet, or whatever animal you like to pet. I mean hey if you like alligators that's **cool. One day** you could pet them, maybe own one! Regardless, **there are** countless things left waiting for you to accomplish. You **are** here. You have read this, and I hope it helps you in some way. Please. I've been there, I'm still a kid. And even when I have my bad days, I'm always looking for better ones because they are out there...they have to be and that's what keeps me going. I hope it can help you keep going as well. In case you haven't been told yet, I love you. You are so incredibly loved. You are worthy. You are strong. You can do it. I am so, so fucking proud of you. And I hope you keep going. If not for yourself, do it for me. The person typing this believes in you and I hope you start to believe in yourself as well.

To: Jack

I'm moving to Berlin in less than a week and it was time to start packing my room. I found the rose you bought me the last time we were together in Spain. I saved it in a small jar to keep it safe from crumbling. I carried that damn thing across Spain, England, and the US. I'm happy I did. 2018 feels like so long ago. We don't talk anymore. It's partially my fault because I pushed you away when I went to college. And it's partially the pandemic. I often wonder what would have happened between us if we lived together like we planned last summer. This is something I was hoping I could tell you in person, but I'm not sure I'll get the chance to do that, given the state of the world. I try not to live with regret and so far in my adult life, despite everything I've been through, I haven't. My experiences, both negative and positive, are things I cherish as they have brought me exactly to where I am at this moment. However, there is one thing I regret, and that's declining the offer you gave me the last time we saw one another. I regret that I didn't stay when you asked. I'm so happy for the life you've built these last two years and I truly wish you and Mae the best. But realizing all these years later how I felt about you has been weighing heavily on me. You were the first adult choice I was presented with and I chose wrong. I wonder often about what my life would look like if I had decided to spend it with you, or at least try to. I'm sorry I was scared to take that chance with you. I miss you, I miss how close we used to be, and I'm sorry I took our friendship for granted. I'm sorry we never talked about those nights which might have saved us both a lot of grief. It's too late now and a bit selfish of me to tell you this all now, but I need to tell you at least once. I love you.

To: Ben

I forgive you.

To: My Parents

I am trying to grow in an environment that I have outgrown. I
know you will never understand this, but I am writing this letter
imagining that you are the parents that will actually take the
time to really listen to the words that I sit here and type. You are
trying to mold me to fit into the future YOU both wanted.
Choosing the length of my hair, my future, my values, beliefs,
and needs. I know you have both tried so hard so that I wouldn't
have to struggle for an education and a future like you did and I
am thankful for that. What I need you to realize is that I am now
struggling to reach that bar that you have put out of my reach.
Paying for my school fees does not mean that I have to pay you
back for the degree that YOU wanted. You are punishing me
every time I try to reach and fail for that bar. When in reality,
that bar is rotting away with time because it was what you
wanted to achieve and failed to.

To: My Kids

I have thrown away that bar that was set generations above me.
It was getting too high as each generation expected more than
what was achieved during their own. I want you to live your life.
Yes, I want you to make the most of every opportunity but I
won't ever set that bar for you. Not now, not ever. You need to
set that bar for yourself. If it's still too high, you are allowed to
lower it because you are already doing more than what you need
to do on this earth. You are free to grow out of an environment
that you are too small for.

To: A

It's taken me a while to figure it out, or maybe I haven't even figured it out. It's taken me a while to admit this - and this is as close as I'll get to it - you wouldn't read this, but I love you.

To: Those Of You Whose Hearts Are Too Big

I remember growing up, people always told me how amazing it was to have a heart like mine. A heart that always saw the good in everyone, no matter how big or small. A heart that always forgave quickly and held no grudges. A heart that loved fiercely as if it were my only reason for breathing. A heart that always took in others' pain & housed it as if it were my own. But now after 26 years on this earth, I feel as if this is the cruelest gift anyone could ever give me. A heart that saw the good, but overlooked the bad, and tried to understand the actions of those who hurt me with their hands and cut me with their words. A heart that forgave quickly, and made it too easy for them to continue to do it time and time again. They knew my feet would be rooted to the spot and I would not leave. A heart, that once it felt that connection, dove headfirst into love, not caring how that person felt about me and burned with a passion of a thousand suns. A heart, that just wanted to help heal those with a broken light, so it always ushered in the pain & trauma of others. Because it believed if it could just help, even the tiniest bit, it would be worth it to be broken in the end. I want to take this heart, pull it from my chest and bury it so no one else may ever find it. So no one else may ever have to experience what it is to have a heart like this. One that brings so much joy, light, compassion, and love wherever it goes. One that reaches out and helps change others, and shows them a true kind of love. But a heart that often forgets how magical it is and lets others leave a new scar upon it. One that no longer believes is special and gets trampled on. A heart that is tired of beating alone.

To: My Abuser

I was only a child. If I rely on the pieces of empty memories, I can come to the conclusion that I was around the age of five or six. Yet, part of me believes it happened more than once. I don't remember it all. What I recall comes back into my mind at the worst times. I remember you, your crystal blue eyes, your cigarette smoke-stained breath, your pores reeking of alcoholism. I remember the sweat on your skin. The lust in your eyes. The lust you had for a child. You were a grown man. A grown man with four of his own kids. My dad was your best friend. You lived across the street. We trusted you. I trusted you. You pinned my small wrists down onto your bed. The bed you shared with your wife. The bed your children climbed into at night when they were scared. You forced yourself onto me, your hot breath leaving stains on my skin that I cannot wash off even twelve years later. Your calloused fingers, soaked in sin. You moved away the next year. I did not tell anyone until ten years later. You still walk free. You are still a father. You are still a husband, to your third wife. I cannot forget what you did, I am just beginning to remember. No matter where you go, no matter how far you run, your calloused fingers - they will always be soaked in sin. Your victim, who is now seventeen, is learning to use her voice. And she is not afraid to use it.

To: The People I Love Most

I hope you are getting through all the battles you aren't telling
me about...I love you.

To: Ethan

I want to marry you one day. I've known you for almost 12 years now and I have never not loved you. From a childish crush at summer hangouts to falling in love with you over 5-hour phone calls and warm hugs. I've never even kissed you, yet I know you are the person I'll choose every time. I've fallen for others, dated and smiled, yet my love for you has never changed. You never cease to amaze me. With eyes of sea green, coffee curls, and a crooked smile, I'll never stop loving you. One day <3

To: Mom

As you said I was your daughter my heart started to hurt. The thought of me being a boy never crossed your mind, and yet it's all I could ever think about. I hated my body. I wanted to be handsome. I wanted my hair short. I wanted to look masculine. I wanted to be a boy, and yet you never noticed. Even when I said I wanted to be a boy, all it ever was to you was a phase. I wished you'd see me as a boy. I know you won't ever see it clearly, so I've given up. I am a boy, even if you don't see it, and I'm proud.

To: Future Archeologists And Curious Aliens

Did we make it? If we didn't, what got to us first? Nuclear war or climate change? Since our fashion today feels like decade-specific nostalgia trends, what is considered new fashion in your time? Was the last war fought for wealth and land or unpolluted resources? Did we ever find out who Banksy was? How long did it take humanity to stop trying? Were there still people fighting till the end? Did Disney continue making those god-awful live-action remakes? Is the internet still around so you can watch our history? I bet we made your job pretty easy. How much of the decline was recorded, do you think? If you are an alien, I'm glad we weren't alone. Are there any flowers left?

To: Younger Me

Stop letting everyone take pieces of you to make themselves feel whole. The things that happened to you weren't your fault no matter what someone tells you. Yes, it does hurt and yes you are allowed to feel that hurt but don't sit and drown in it. You know you deserve so much better. Keep that spark of life lit inside yourself kid.

To: Dad

My whole life you told me I was a mini-you. I was a people person, just like you. I was creative, just like you. I could feel the music and understand it, just like you. You told me every day I was just like you. When I meet people sometimes you wouldn't even say my name, just say "this is mini-me." My name didn't matter because I was basically just you. I was your favorite person because I was just like you. But Dad, I'm nothing like you. I would never leave my family, just like you did. I would never forget my daughter's birthday, just like you did. I would never have a secret affair, just like you did. I always felt I looked up to you, but now I feel as though I'm looking down. Down at a man who is crumbling. Down at a man I don't recognize. I fear that one day, I'll look in the mirror and not see myself. Only see little you.

To: Andrew

I still write our initials in the sand every time I go to the beach because deep down there is a part of me that will never let us go.

To: An Old Friend

Maybe I learned to love from your monster high skateboard that I used to try so hard to impress you on, down your street.
Sometimes I forget how much I miss you, your awkward parents, and your cats.
Will I see you again?
It'll always sting. And I'll never be able to fix all of your problems like you did mine. I never really told you I loved you frequently enough.
But I did, and I do.
You always tried to show me your favorite Mitski songs when she wasn't cool.
I always tried to show you Phoebe Bridgers songs that I liked.
But we never listened to each other's suggestions until years later when I didn't ride your monster high skateboard anymore.
Could we talk about them now? I miss you.

To: Anyone Who Needs To Hear It

I have a feeling all the letters you will receive are going to be more like confessions and people admitting how sad and deeply unhappy they are. Simply because a lot of people don't have an outlet, so writing an anonymous letter that could one day be shared with the world seems like the only option when you need someone to talk to. However, I have something different to say. I love you. I love the world. I love everyone so much and so hard I often don't know what to do with it. I love when my neighbors laugh or sing. I love when an emergency vehicle comes through and everyone pulls over and life just stops for a second. I love when something bad happens and people just shrug and go "it's okay." I love when someone takes care of another sick person knowing they will also get sick. There is so much beauty in everyday life. We often yearn for a better afterlife that we forget to make the life we are living now, worth it.

To: Anyone Whoever Decides To Become A Parent

At every chance, remind your child every day how much you love them. Because growing up watching everyone around you be loved and accepted all the while you get nothing, is more painful than you could ever imagine. Just make sure you mean it because what hurts more than never hearing it, is being told despite knowing full well it is a lie.

To: My Father

I was watching this show today, and this gay guy was getting married and his dad was walking him down the aisle. I fully tore up and started crying because I realized you're never going to walk me down the aisle. Never going to accept me for who I am, and that hurts so fucking much. When I watch shows and I see dads being overprotective over their daughters and all that, it hurts because we don't have that. We don't have anything. You focus on your new family so it probably doesn't bother you. But it bothers me, dad. So how am I supposed to deal with the fact that telling you I'm gay, means losing the tiny sorry excuse of a relationship we have left. It shouldn't have to be this hard. You're my dad. You're supposed to love me no matter what.

To: A Future Writer

A pen. A piece of paper. Another piece of paper. Think. Think more. Think again. Write down a subject. Write down a theme. Write down a time period. Create characters. Create conversations. Create stories. A book. Maybe short. But made by you. This is the sign you should write a story. Creativity feeds our souls. There is no such thing as failing in doing so. The phrase 'try again' is there for a reason. Now go!

To: Sun

Even though you stopped bringing me sunshine years ago, I stuck through the cloudy weather that followed us everywhere. I got used to the rain falling in our lives. I could not even tell you when our last good day was. If I thought hard enough about it I bet it was a nice, warm day. We were probably starting our day with a talk on the couch bantering about what embarrassing things we did the night before. I loved nights with you. Even after the sun went away, I was our moon that shined enough for the both of us. For a while at least. After the banter, we probably got in your car – dressed in baggy sweatpants and t-shirts that relieved our suffocating skin from the tight outfits we danced in the night before. Chicken biscuits for breakfast, of course, was the next stop. Even if we were too hungover to eat our food, we had to go, simply for the environment on the way there. It felt so safe and free in your car. Even though you drove like our safety and freedom could end at any moment. I just know the moment your engine turned over and the car started, the music would be too loud and good to have any other thought go through my mind, other than what lyric was up next to scream in delight at the top of our lungs. The windows were always down, too. I love how vulnerable the opened car windows made us to other people on the streets. Though you were the sun to my moon for so many years, being vulnerable was not something we cared to master in our friendship. We hardly even hugged. But that did not bother either of us, because the bond we had was so strong that no physical touch would compare to our energies bouncing off each other from a distance. Anyway, that was probably how the start of our last good day went. It's a weird feeling, us not being in each other's lives anymore. It is not a bad feeling – but it is not a good feeling either. You knew everything about me and I could read your mind with just a facial expression. But in order for you to remind me of sunshine again, we need to be apart. It just got too hard. Our friendship is so much prettier looking back on it, rather than living in it. It makes me miss you the most, but I am grateful I have all those good days to look back on to bring me a little sunshine. I love you

To: The Spider That Sits In The Corner Of My Room

I really do feel sorry for you and everything I put you through.
The slippers I threw at you and the screams when I first saw you
but now you bring me peace. You're the only one who has seen
me dance around my room to Hannah Montana and cry at Pacey
and Joey's edits on youtube. You know me better than anyone
else. I named you, by the way, you looked like a Sid. If that's not
your name please let me know. I'd feel stupid if I continued to
call you the wrong name. I hope I don't scare you like you
sometimes scare me when you move. I hope you consider me a
friend too. I apologize for the screaming of music at 3 pm on a
Sunday afternoon and the mess that I call my room. I just can't
believe I was the human you chose to scare.

To: My Younger Self

When looking at myself now, I know you would be terrified that I ever even thought about leaving. When a bag of popcorn and a fire outside with my family was enough. Enough to feel like there was a reason to be here and keep on living. I am okay, albeit. I am fine. But, why do I not feel that anymore? Why do I not look at a sunset the same or want to catch every firefly I see? Why do I not smear s'mores over my siblings' faces or yell when they beat me in Mario Kart? Where did that happy person go? Why was it so easy? Why did I want to leave that neverland of youth and grow up into a person I barely recognize as me? I don't feel alive anymore. I'm just here. So that's why I am hoping for something. Hoping that I figure it out. Hoping that curiosity is enough to keep me here and wonder what satisfaction I could have from staying. I want to be the person you could smile to and know that they're happy because I want to be happy. So, I'll stay. For you, my dear. I'll stay and try. Because I love you. To the stars and beyond.

To: You

I thank the universe for giving me an opportunity to experience you.

To: Another Stage Of Grief

"Maybe in another lifetime…" This line shouldn't even exist. You see, I would say this to myself, and it pulled me into a black hole of denial. Maybe you will care about me, maybe I will bump into you, maybe you'll show up at my house, maybe you'll text me… You never did. You broke my heart more than anyone has, and I blame this line.

To: Men

A no means fucking no. Screams mean no. Crying means no. Pushing away means no. Even a nod means no! Get that through your fucking head. Innocent girls, women, and even men are now scarred for life because someone didn't care and didn't understand what it meant. Now they are expected to live life as if nothing happened. Like they weren't a victim of sexual assault. It will affect them for years to come. Some have many flashbacks. Some have nightmares. Some are triggered by a single touch, word, or even a picture. It's so sad how someone's life can be changed forever because of it.

To: Caleb

Hi, thank you for driving all the way up here to hang out with me
for a day. It made me so very happy. I really like you a lot and
you probably don't feel the same way, but that's okay. As long as
you stay in my life, it will be okay. See you on Thursday!

To: Cancer

I was 7.
7 years old.
I was happy. Not a care in the world...until one day you met my mom.
Why did you choose her? Was it because she was so beautiful? Kind? Caring? Funny? Or was it because you don't care about who you hurt? At one point we thought you had left us alone...never to be seen again. But my god we were so wrong. You came back into our lives smashing down the front door and breaking anything that got in your way. Until the only thing that was in your way was the hospital bed. My mom spent those months knowing she would never get to see me grow into the woman I am today. That she would never go to my prom, or hold me in her arms whilst I cry about another silly boy breaking my heart. You just didn't care, did you? Sometimes I cry myself to sleep knowing I can't just tell her about my day. All of this...because of you. I hope you're happy. I know I certainly am...making my mom proud each day. Goodbye, I hope we never hear from each other again.

To: "Closet"

I don't wanna be in here anymore, everything feels weird and lonely right now. I wish I could live my true self. I wish I could live without fear.

To: The Ocean

I just wanted to let you know that you've saved me. You've saved me a thousand times over again and will always be my happy place. The smell of the air, the sound of the waves, the feeling of the sand on my feet. It's like an instant rush of relief. It doesn't matter how hot or cold it is, sunny or cloudy, you can make my day better regardless. Maybe it's because I've been a stroll away from you my whole life. It could be the countless hours I've spent swimming, boating, windsurfing, sailing, and floating in your presence. There have been countless happy memories made with family, friends, pets, and the occasional turtle to boot. Some people believe you're destructive and dangerous. They believe you hold only aggression and cause fear. However, I feel the love radiating from your waves. I will always come back to you. Don't worry, to me you'll forever be my home <3

To: Natasha

Hey, I know writing a letter to you is so cliche but I really could never say this to your face without my heart racing and palms sweating...you are one of the most beautiful souls I know. I envy your free-spirited mind and the way you see things in the world. They were right when they said there are no two people...there could never be two of you – no one could be as kind, loving, smart, and as beautiful as you. My heart almost bursts every time I see you...and I mean that quite literally. No one makes me feel as important as you do. You helped me find myself when I thought all hope was lost. If you ever figure out who wrote this, give me a call. Lots and lots of love, hugs, and cute frog tiktoks.

To: The Baby I Never Knew

I am so sorry. I wish I had known. I wish I would've made different choices. You would have been so loved and there wouldn't have been a day where you weren't in my arms. I thought I had known heartbreak, but losing you was the most painful thing I have ever experienced. I was an idiot and it's all my fault that you weren't able to join us in the world. I mourn you every day. It's been nearly 2 years and my heart is still in shreds. You were loved, you are still loved and I'm so sorry my body wasn't strong enough. I'm so sorry you felt my body wasn't safe enough for you. I will never forgive myself or forget you.

To: Everyone Who's Hurting Alone

I'm struggling. Alone. I don't tell anyone, they don't ask, and the world still spins; time continues. My parents fight and bicker all the time. I sit on the top of my stairs to make sure nothing gets physical. It did once. Other times, I comfort my siblings. We shut my door, turn a movie up loud, and pretend like it's not affecting us. It does. Sometimes I can't breathe. I hate summer, I hate putting on a swimsuit. I hate how I look from all angles. I hate the pictures that are taken of me. Everyone tells me how slim I am, but I don't see it. My shoulders are too broad, my stomach not flat enough, my thighs too fat, my jaw not sharp enough, my nose too big, my boobs too small. I hate when people tell me I'm pretty. I feel like they're lying, and I can't help but feel like that. I have only two friends I'm close with. My phone stays mostly silent. It could go hours upon hours without ringing, and I don't want to be the one texting first all the time. It makes me feel like I'm being annoying. I feel like a burden most of the time. Parties and celebrations scare me, as do conversations with people I don't know. Large groups make me nervous. I don't know what to do when someone cries, and hugging isn't an option for me. Touch makes me drawback, and I don't know why. I cringe away from embraces, even from the people I trust the most. I can tell it hurts them. I feel guilty most of the time, but still, I don't initiate affection. I show affection through sarcasm. It's my shield. My sister picks at her fingers as an anxiety tic. Sometimes they bleed. It's no secret she has anxiety, that she stresses easily. My mom calls me "her easy child," her "happy child."- Because there's nothing wrong with me. Because I'm a student-athlete who made varsity in freshman year, who was MVP two years in a row, who gets good grades, who does work without complaining, who is...normal. Who doesn't have any mental illnesses because that's impossible as she's supposed to be "easy."- She's supposed to be "happy." The truth is, I'm struggling. Alone. I don't tell anyone, they don't ask, and the world still spins; time continues.

To: Veldman

Dear V, I am so unbelievably sorry. When we had met in 2018, I was in tears with how much love I still had yet to give you. I knew you were leaving on deployment soon and I said I would wait and you told me not to. Then the pandemic hit – and you were gone longer than you said you would be. And I fell in love again...with someone else. I don't remember what led us back to each other, but I know that when we met again we were different people. Over dinner, I told you that I hadn't waited and you told me that you wished you said you loved me then. After dinner, we shared a moment that felt like how I felt when we first met and I continued feeling that way for you. I was going to put my life away to continue living it with you, but I had to take a step back. I wanted to work on my existing relationship because leaving with you didn't feel right. I ended up getting married to my now-husband. I really didn't want to tell you...and part of me wishes I hadn't. You are the one who got away. I wish I had more time with you in the beginning.

To: Dad

Hi Dad. This is your daughter. I have never met you and you have never met me. I think about you often. I wonder if I have any characteristics like you. I wonder if I act like you. I don't even know if you even know that I exist. My mom told me that in 1999, you wanted nothing to do with me. When she found out she was pregnant with me, you wanted nothing to do with me. Or her. Why? Why give up on us? I only found out your name when I was 18. I searched you up on Facebook and found out that you lived in the same town as me. Who knows how many times I've seen you and just not realized that it was you. My fiancé and I are planning a wedding and it's so hard because I don't have a dad to dance with. I don't have a dad to walk me down the aisle. And that hurts. I will never reach out to you personally. So I write this letter to show you how I really feel. I'm not so mad or sad anymore. It's just what I'm used to. No dad. No father figure. Nothing. And it hurts to see that you have a family. With kids and a wife. Were we not good enough? As I wrap this letter up I wonder, if you do remember me, what do you think about me? Do you think about the life we could've had? Do you regret not being in my life or staying with my mom? Having to even write this letter is such a bummer. Hope you're happy.

To: Margaret

Dear Margaret, I miss you every single day. It's been hard to cope with loss, especially since I loved you so much. Everything I do reminds me of you. The smell of the flowers in the garden, the hammock in the backyard, and the clothes that I wear. If you were still here today, I would give you the everlasting love that you deserve. I know that so many people miss you so much, and I wish you could see how many people love you. I wish that I could've been there in your final moments to tell you that I love you and that it's okay. I still have your birthday card on my dresser, the one I was never able to give to you. I'll love you forever.

To: Lola

I don't think I can ever fully describe you in words. The words I want to use don't exist, none are beautiful enough. There's nothing about you that I don't like. I am completely captivated by your existence. As much as I hate the world, I have to admit, it's not as bad, just because: it has you in it.

To: Dad

It was unexpected and I'm sorry. If I had known it was my last chance to say farewell, I would have picked up. But that's grief. And with that regret, I blame myself and wonder, what if? What if I had said I love you...one last time. Nothing would be different. I'd still miss you and you still would be gone. And that's what grief is. A flip of the coin that only has one ending. So, for something I never got to say to you, pops, I love you.

To: My Habits

You came back today...and yesterday...the day before that too. You were like a haunted hand that dragged me back down into the dark lake that sat awaiting my return. I cried again. Not because of how I was ashamed, but because I was surprised. You see I thought I was free from you and yet I find myself back in your grasp. Even my best friend noticed my arms. Her mouth doesn't drop anymore nor do any tears from the corners of her eyes as they used to, because she knew. She knew it would happen. Again, and again. They all did.

To: Gavin

I miss you every day. I work at the gas station you used to go to all the time now. I'm thinking about quitting because every time I drive by or look out into the street I think about what you must have been thinking when they hit you. Were you excited to go to the store and see your friends? Angry it took so long for your bike to start that morning? Annoyed about having to work that day? Happy to be going somewhere? Would you still be here if I'd just offered you a ride that morning instead of going back to sleep? What would you be like today? Would you still be easygoing and happy to make new friends, would you have a girlfriend, would you still be living in our house? It's only been two years but I miss you all the time, I wish I'd gotten to say sorry. You were a good brother and I wish I had told you that. But I don't get any of that. So I hope there's a heaven you're in right now, and I hope you're fishing at your favorite spot up there.

To: Mom and Dad

I'm pangender, aromantic, and feminamoric. I'm sorry I never told you. I think being in the closet is nice. I know that I am in control of who I tell, and that brings me comfort. I am not Christian, like you raised me, and am currently trying to figure out if I believe in anything or I'm just an atheist. I love you guys, you mean the world to me, but I don't fully trust you with my identity yet. I'll let you know when I do.

To: My Past Self

Hi, I know that you're so overwhelmed and feel like you have to be this smart girl that does big things and makes everyone proud. I know you feel like you have to be there for everyone even when you aren't feeling the greatest and I know that you feel like you don't deserve to be sad because of how your upbringing was. Please allow yourself to feel. Don't be afraid to talk to people about how you're feeling because eventually, it's going to be too much for you. Stop holding things in. I wish that I had someone to tell me that because I have had some really rough patches. That's why I want you to take this advice and find an outlet for your thoughts. You'll be okay.

To: My Uber Driver

I did not appreciate it when I was crying in the backseat on the way home while you were playing Dance Monkey on repeat.

To: Anyone

I hope that you make the right choices. Do it. Text them first, tell them how you feel. Let them know that you are there. Make sure they're ok. Joke around with them, show them how funny you can be. Talk about anything, find something you have in common. Just do it, don't be afraid. Don't shy away because you aren't sure. Just do it. I want you to be happy and enjoy where you are. Don't expect too much because that's not how life works. Not everything goes your way. Expect the unexpected. But be happy doing it. Live how you want. I hope that this letter finds you well, and I hope you are where you want to be. If not then I hope you get there soon. I love you, and I mean it. Just know there is someone rooting for you on the other side of the page.

To: Myself

And even after everything; life is still so beautiful!

To: Sammy The Sloth

I apologize for ignoring you for so long. You were a gift, a stuffed animal from someone who used to love me. I used to love you, just like how I used to love him. For such a sweet gift, it's weird to think the one who gifted you has changed so much. I want to hold you close and to fall asleep with you in my arms...but I can't. He has tainted you. He has tainted my memories. You'd be glad to know that despite the hell he has put me through, I have been getting better. It is still a work in progress, but I promise you, once I am able to overcome this entire mess, you will be in my arms again. It's just hard sometimes. I really don't want to be near anything that could remind me of him. I had my happiest memories with him, but I also had my most painful moments because of him. I'm upset it took me so long to see him for what he is. He never did try to push through...did he? I put so much effort in for it all to end in failure. I'm sorry, Sammy. I hope I can love you again eventually.

To: Dad

I remember so vividly the first time I had felt so unbelievably betrayed by you. I was sitting on my back porch on my twelfth birthday. My friends were inside, laughing and playing games at my party. It was late at night, and I still hadn't heard from you at all. I sat there, on the porch stairs with my phone in my hands, and I cried. I cried because you used to be there for me. I cried because you made me a promise that you would never leave me behind. I cried because I knew you were spending time with your fiancé and new little girl. I'm still crying. I cry because no matter how good my mom and stepdad treat me, no matter how much they love me and take care of me and are the best parents anyone could ask for, I still yearn for my dad back. I just want my dad.

To: Santa

I want a pony for Christmas.

To: A Stranger

When you see me, remember me. Whether we exchange meaningless pleasantries at a café or study each other's expressions across a subway; remember me. Remember me as the joyful girl with happy eyes, rather than the broken doll with a worthless expression. Remember me as the healthy and energetic body, rather than the hollow and empty presence. Remember me as a young youthful teenager with an effortless smile, rather than the torn apart mannequin with a stone face. Remember me as who I wish to be, rather than who I am. So when you pass me in the hall or lock eyes with me on the train, study me, and remember me for the person I wish to be. Remember me. Remember me. Remember me.

To: Harry

I hope we last forever.

To: Everyone

Do what makes your soul happy.

To: My Rapist

Ever since I was a little girl I was always warned about the big scary men that lurked in the shadows that would hurt you if you were walking alone at night. The thing I was not told about is that the men who can hurt you aren't always big and scary and they don't lurk in the shadows. Sometimes you meet them at Christian camp and they smell good and have nice smiles. They are kind and they are your friend.

I was 12 years old when I met you. When we left camp that year we stayed in contact, only building our friendship for years. The next time I saw you in person I was 14. It was Christmas Eve and there was a bad snowstorm. You invited me over to your apartment. I felt safe, you were my friend, and it was only a block away from my grandma's house.

I was wrong to feel safe, and I was wrong to trust you. You weren't my friend at all. You were the man I was told about my whole life. The man who would hurt me worse than anyone had before. I always imagined losing my virginity to be a special moment with a man I loved, not you holding me down and not stopping as I screamed no over and over through tears. You finished with me and kicked me out of your apartment into the cold. I walked a block back to my grandma's and ate dinner with my family like the worst thing that's ever happened to me didn't just happen. 3 months later I found out I was carrying your baby. I was 14 carrying my rapist's baby. I kept that baby because of my family's religion. I couldn't get rid of it. Our son is now 2 years old and looks more and more like you every day. I assure you, I will do absolutely everything in my power to make sure he is nothing like you. While you rot in prison, MY son and I will be growing and healing together. He is a miracle and will never think otherwise.

-The girl who survived you

To: The One I Think I Love

Hey, I think I'm in love with you but I don't really know because I haven't seen you for the last two years. Covid has messed up high school. I don't remember how you act, what you sound like, or even if you'll be my friend when school starts again. It's so hard to not see you every day at school like I used to. I used to take one route in the hall just so I can see you. I used to come five minutes early to school because my locker was so close to yours that I could just talk to you. And that made me so happy.

To: Jamie

Why are your eyes on me instead of her? She's pouring her heart into what you two have and I myself have someone else in mind; why do I still catch you gazing towards me in that case? I care about Olivia more than anyone and that girl deserves nothing but love. You know that, Jamie? Why are you giving her anything but that? Why are you giving her uncertainty? Fear? Thoughts of worthlessness and not being good enough? Why are you giving such a pure soul any of that? I'm focusing on my own soulmate. It's he who stays in my head all day, not you. I want nothing more than to be in his arms...and yet I always catch you staring at me. I always catch you calling me beautiful and insisting you take more photos of us together. I always recall each time you ask me to go watch the sunset with you. Even star-gazing from time to time as well. I remember each time you complimented my outfit and each time you played with my hair. I always notice you seem to care about what's going on in my life just a little bit more than you should as a casual acquaintance. All I want is for you to turn the other way. Give what you give me to her. Love her the way you want to love me. You two would be a fairytale come true. Ours is one of confusion, lack of reciprocation, and guilt. Please turn the other way because a girl as perfect as Olivia comes once in a lifetime.

To: Dad

Hi. It's almost been 8 years. Half of my life. I miss you and I'm scared of what's to come. I'm scared of how many cancer genes I have in me. I'm scared that I'm going to do something to cause a reaction from them. I'm scared that the same could happen to my siblings. I'm scared. I've also been thinking about what it would be like if you were still here. Or what you would think about how I turned out. I don't think you'd be super happy. I'm not what you wanted. "The perfect conservative, Christian father is severely disappointed in his queer, left-leaning daughter." That would about summarize it. I'm scared mom knows. I'm scared that she won't accept it and she'll never talk to me again. I'm scared that if that happens, I'll never talk to my brother again. I still love you, and I hope you still love me.

To: Taylor Swift

I really need that 10-minute version of All Too Well to come out so I can have a new song to cry to, thanks!

To: You

I miss you every day. The smallest things remind me of you, but the moon the most of them all. We made this promise that if we ever missed each other, we would look at the moon because no matter what's going on, how far apart we are, we will always be looking at the same moon. I hear you're with her now. I always knew you would end up with her. Her fresh blonde hair and contagious smile.

I hear how you laugh with her.

I see how you look at her.

I know the words you say to her.

Because once you said them all to me. That didn't matter though, did it? Because I'm just a girl. Some random girl you thought was a good idea to date.

But it was always her wasn't it? Now I look back at it. All the time we walked hand in hand, I saw you glance at her. You never looked at me like that. I saw the way you laughed with her. Never like that with me.

The hardest one to see is the way you love her. I thought you could never love another like me? That was true, yes, because you love her more. You love her more than me.

To: Future Me

Are you still scared to fall in love? Are you in love? You're 25 right now and you've never given it a chance. You feel as if no one will love you because of your health so you don't even bother opening up to anyone. Right now, I have end-stage 4 chronic kidney disease. The one kidney I have is failing, barely holding on. To be honest, I feel like I'm barely holding on too. The only thoughts that consume my mind recently are "when will I find the one?" Tell me why I'm in the process of choosing a dialysis option, but I still continue to daydream about when I'll meet the one. I guess I crave it so bad because I've never been in a relationship. I feel like no one's going to love me because who would want to commit to a girl whose second home is the hospital? People enjoy being carefree, and with me, well you can't afford to be carefree. Everyone keeps telling me that if it's really meant to be he's going to love me for me and love everything about me. They tell me I have nothing to worry about but I'm so scared. I have so many scars on my body from surgeries. Who can love that? What if they get scared...I don't know. Every guy I've told so far has only wanted to remain as friends. What if I never fall in love? I hope you find everything you're searching for. Maybe I've truly waited this long for something special but who knows, maybe I'm meant to be alone. Only time will tell. I hope your relationship with your sister is better, I hope you're still best friends with your best friend.

To: My Wallet

I really just bought Wattpad premium and I'm not even mad about it.

To: A "Family Friend"

I don't play 21 questions anymore because of one simple
question. When did you lose your virginity? It's a trivial question
for most, but the fear that builds up in me trying to find a
different answer to the question than 4 is hard. It's a confusing
answer for someone who doesn't quite understand what you did
to me for all those years. Hopefully, you see this someday and
know that I will never forgive you.

To: Him

Do you remember the day we laid in that tall grassy field, with
the sky looking so blue it could be an endless bright ocean with
clouds? Do you remember when you gave a white weed flower
and said, "Daisy for you! I know it's not a real daisy but I believe
it's as pretty as one and deserves the name." Do you remember
when you looked at me in 3rd period and said everything was
going to be okay when I was having a panic attack? Do you
remember when you and G were trying to teach me Spanish
while I was teaching you guys German? Do you remember when
you used to just be the boy in the back until I met you, and called
you scary because of your height? I never knew you and I never
thought I would get to. I see you every day in the halls. In class, I
say hi sometimes but you seem to say nothing. I miss you. I really
do. I miss your smile, laughter, calling me short. I just miss you.
Do you remember me?

To: Them

I wish I never wasted all that time loving you when I could have been learning to love myself.

To: Every Human

I've spent years of my life worrying about the way I look. The way my body looks and the way my face looks. Hours and hours of sitting in front of a mirror looking at myself from every angle possible to view with the human eye. I've cried over myself, and I've laughed over myself. But even with all the hours and hours of studying myself, I've also been wasting my years, days, and minutes. Really any amount of time, trying my absolute best to avoid a mirror or anything that shows my reflection at all. I became scared of my reflection. Hating yourself to a point where you have to avoid yourself is a horrible way to live life. I've finally understood that. I now walk in front of my mirror every morning and say to myself, "you are beautiful and you deserve love." I say this because even though I might not believe it, practice makes perfect. If I practice saying that, I might actually become it. In all seriousness, everyone was made for a purpose. You mean something. You may not know that meaning yet, but you will find it. I'm still searching and struggling every day, but time heals, and time will heal me if I allow it. Find a saying. Maybe mine, or maybe your own. Make it a habit to repeat this message to yourself every day. You can say it in the morning when you're getting ready, or maybe at school when you get nervous, or at any random time when you need a little truth and pick me up. You are beautiful. In every way. Work on yourself. Work on your heart. Have a wonderful life.
Love, your friend always and forever.

To: My Future Self

I hope you're happier.

To: Mom

When will the tears stop? When will the pain subside? When will I see you again? You always had the answers to every question, and now I lay awake at night thinking about the time that has passed without you, and the many questions left unanswered. Often I find myself drifting back to the memories of the last few weeks I had with you. The weeks I cling onto and hope you don't remember. The images of you still haunt my mind. You, my protector. You, my biggest fan. You, my best friend. I sat there night and day watching your face, hoping for a glimpse of you remaining. Night and day I listened to the machines around me, hoping for proof that you were fighting on the inside. Instead, I witnessed your pain and suffering. Instead, I listened to the doctors tell me there was no option left. I cried and screamed at your bedside, hoping you'd hear. I begged the universe for just one more miracle, one more time you'd be brought back to me. I knew your soul was in there, fighting like you always did. But I had seen it, your body had taken all it could and there was no coming back. They gave me a choice, allow the inevitable or give you some dignity. I waited, I listened to the pain of others as they wept over you. And then the day came where the decision had to be made. It was that day that my heart shattered. I couldn't bring myself to leave your side because I knew that once I did, it would all be over. I went to a home that would never be filled with your joy and ignited with your passion. I stepped back into a life that didn't feel like my own anymore. Am I ever going to be able to live a life without you?

To: Richard

Richard, your name held so much power over me for so many years. I would see it and break, I would hear it and shudder, I'd close my eyes and be back there. In that room where you broke my ribs, eye socket, and jaw. The room where you raped me. A 16-year-old girl who worked at a village pub. You will never understand what you took from me that night. What I can make you understand though is how you did not break me. I love myself and I love my life. Your name holds no more power over me. It's the name of a weak and disgusting man who I will never let enter my mind after this letter. You are not worthy of my forgiveness or even compassion and I hope the feeling of regret and shame lives within you for the rest of your life. I am powerful and you are nothing.

To: Tyler

I still think about you almost every day. You're out there somewhere making memories. You're seeing the same sunset as me; the same moon and the same rain. I'm making memories of my own too. Sometimes I can't even believe that you're not here to live them with me. I look for you in everyone I meet. I look for the same connection we shared, but I haven't found it and I'm scared I never will...they don't laugh with me in awkward moments, or tell stories in a hushed voice even if there is no one around, or stare deep into my soul. I still say to myself, well maybe someday...someday we'll cross paths again. Though, the chances of that happening are one in a million...but the spark I felt with you was one in a million too, so who knows...maybe someday.

To: Dad

It's my birthday in a few days. I'll be turning 18! Yep. Your daughter is finally an adult. Why do you care more about alcohol than me? Can you celebrate alcohol's birthday? Can you watch alcohol grow? Can you learn about alcohol, your favorite music, hobbies, etc.? I hate who it turns you into. You turn into someone I don't know. I know we're not in contact now, but I still think about you every day, even after everything you didn't do for me. After every hurtful, drunken word you spat. I know you won't wish me a happy birthday, and I've come to terms with that. The really sad thing is, I don't want to speak to you, I want you to speak to me. I want you to care enough about me to sort things out between us as a normal father would do. I still love you, I always will but I'll always hate you too. For what you put me and my mother through. I miss you. The sober you, and I know I'll never get him back. I hope alcohol's favorite color is blue and alcohol's favorite movie is Beetlejuice. I hope alcohol thanks you for wishing them a happy 18th. I hope alcohol can fill some holes that I couldn't.

To: Zach

Zach, I am so fucking in love with you. You are a constellation of everything I have ever loved. You, my love, are beautiful.

To: My First Ever Puppy Love

There's not a day that goes by where I don't think about you and how everyone lost a soul like you so early. I think about what would happen if I said yes in that little note you gave me, and I wonder what you would be like today. Our time together was so short and I'm going to try every day to never forget your face. We were so small then, we met back in elementary school and you had a crush on me even way back then. I remember wanting to mark the little checkbox that said "yes" and remembering your sweet smile when you handed me the note on the bus before I went home. I remember when I made you laugh, and I remember when you used to make fun of me because someone convinced me not to check the box marked "yes." It's been almost 11 years now and I still wonder what it would've been like if I said yes. I remember after I heard you passed away, I cried and couldn't stop. My mom told me I was the one you liked. My mom told me it was puppy love and I remember crying at school after they announced what happened. I think about you every so often and I wonder what it would've been like if you were able to grow up. I miss you.

To: You, Just Because

I don't know who you are. I don't know what battle you are fighting. I don't know if I can say anything to make your pain stop. But you are beautiful. I don't know you but yet I know that you are a beautiful soul with beautiful ambitions and a beautiful future.

To: My Houseplants

I'm sorry that I don't water you as often as I should, and that I don't notice when the dust collects on your leaves. I try but it is difficult to take care of others when you can just barely take care of yourself. I promise I will try harder.

To: Seth

I'm sorry for pushing you away. I'm sorry because I'm the reason we don't talk. And I'm sorry for having to walk past you and having to pretend we were ever anything. I'm sorry, but I miss you. I miss the head tilt and smile you'd give me when you were right in an argument. I miss eye contact and giggles. I miss messing with you. I miss your blue eyes and blonde hair. I miss the stupid remarks you'd make over every little thing. And I miss having to say "Have a good day" before we left. But I especially miss the way you would look at me. It's my fault, I admit it, but I'm sorry. I hate myself for pushing you away from the second that things got too hard for me. I admit that I was wrong. You were right. Now, please give me the smug smile, knowing you were right.

To: Him

I would live this crazy life 1 million times if it means I get to fall in love with you all over again.

To: Death

"What is the greatest misfortune in life?" Death. Yes, you. You're a thief. You steal not only a man's life but a wife's husband, a child's father, a friend's best mate. You steal people's family and friends, and all we can say is "man, they had a great life." Stealing them at a young age is not only cruel but unfair. They were given a life to fulfill it, and you take it away as if it's nothing. You're a monster, and I will never understand how people are not scared of you. We try giving them peace with a gathering filled with kind words and flowers where we mourn over our loss, but one day those flowers will rot and those words will fade to whispers. You then leave us with their presence, and all we have left are memories. And you know what? We can't do anything about it. We have to eventually accept what we have done and go along with our lives as if nothing happened. You are completely and utterly dark, only leaving shadows wherever you cross. Fuck you.

To: Mary J

I know it's not healthy, but I'm at my happiest with Mary J. Because while in that moment of temporary high, I forget all the things that are going wrong in my life. So I wanna say thank you to Mary J for giving me these moments of temporary happiness. Those moments where I laugh for no reason, feel at peace and feel whole. I love Mary J for all those things but sometimes without her, I feel as though I can't feel happiness, that she's the only one that can bring me that feeling of peace, and I'll admit that scares me a bit.

To: Troy

I'll never not love you, no matter what.

To: My Parents

I forgive you. Not because you earned it, neither did you ever apologize to me. I'm simply letting my soul rest after all this suffering.

To: Zoe

Okay, so I accidentally wrote your name because this was going to be some big sappy confession. But I cringed and went to change it, and now I can't delete it. So I think this is the universe telling me to just tell you. I'm in love with you. God, I am so desperately in love with you. I love the way you cover your mouth when you laugh. I love it when you bring up nerdy facts and then immediately apologize as if I'm not swooning. I love when you throw up peace signs or finger guns every time you don't know what to say. I love the way your eyes turn into raw diamonds when you're in the sunlight. I love that you really don't care what people think about you, as if you know that they aren't worth your time. And I love that you can read a book in a matter of minutes. I fucking love that you are the most authentic person I've ever met. You haven't changed in the years that I have known you at all. Maybe matured, but you're still the awkward, nerdy, adorable girl I've known forever. Zoe, you made me want to get married. You make me have that giddy crush feeling after two years of not having it. You made my friends sick of hearing your name. You made my keyboard remember your name. You make my heart skip beats and my pale face turns scarlet. And, Zoe, if you ever see this letter, or find out that I wrote this, I might die out of humiliation. But I mean every single thing I said. And I'm not taking it back. And I cannot believe it took me six months to admit that I'm in love with you.

To: My Twelve Year Old Self

I'm sorry no one believed you. I'm sorry you thought it was normal. I'm sorry for letting you keep it to yourself. I'm sorry I didn't let you validate our trauma just because some people had it worse. You didn't deserve any of it, and I'm sorry I've kept it to myself until now. It's becoming too heavy; I hope we get better.

To: Millie

I didn't realize love could scare me this much.

To: Tommy

The problem with grief is that it doesn't have an expiration date. There isn't a neat little label stuck to its side, saying, "Here is where it ends." The truth is I'm terrified. It's been months, and I'm still caught in this vicious cycle of mourning you. I know that you're gone. I know you're dead, Tommy. I know it's selfish, but your death just seems so damn unfair. We're just kids. God, we're just teenagers. That's the thing about twins – at least for the two of us. We entered this world together; some twisted part of me hoped we'd leave it together too. I'm learning to function again. I get out of bed. I eat. I sleep too much. It's very hard, however, to live without a heart. Hell, Tommy, you were the embodiment of love. The body goes cold without a heart to pump its blood. It's so cold here. I'm sick, Toms. In the head, in the body. Grief is such a funny thing. There comes a point where both the symptoms of depression are physical and mental. I'm going to die missing you. But for now, this is goodbye. I'm writing this letter for closure. Please understand that I can't keep living like this. It's okay to mourn, I know that. But this? It's gotten to be too much. You'll always be my brother. I know this is self-centered, but I have to let go. For now, this is a temporary goodbye. We'll say hello again one day, I promise. I love you. Wait for me.

To: Those Who Have Lost Themselves

It's okay not to know who you are at this very moment, for one must lose themselves to find themselves again. Our minds are labyrinths, with many turns & endless hallways. The more lost you are, the more you need to search within the confines of your mind. The more you search, you'll see that the answer to finding oneself, is & has always been, within you. Keeping looking within. You can find more than just yourself.

To: Him

Dude, the things I would do to even just spend a second alone
with you.

To: My Last Date

I'm really sorry I turned you down like that. I swear I didn't mean to. I had a great time. You made me smile and laugh like I haven't in a few months. I felt comfortable on a first date for the first time. I really liked it. But I thought I was ready when I wasn't. I wasn't even close. It's been seven months since my last relationship fell to pieces. I thought that was enough time, plenty of time, but I guess it wasn't. I can't stop thinking about her. Whenever I get a cute message like "good morning!" I'm not able to respond. I freeze and just can't make myself do it. I don't want to hurt you so I think it'd be better if we didn't see each other anymore.

: The Reader

I think I'm in love with someone I know I can't be with.

To: Zoe

Hey Zoe, I'm writing this letter anonymously because I don't have the guts to actually write this to you and send it to you. So here it is. Thank you. I'm so grateful that I have a friend like you. We've known each other for so long and you've always helped me and been there for me. You listened to me cry for an hour on the phone last Friday afternoon. I hope this beautiful friendship can last long. And even if we do fall apart, I'll keep our memories in my heart as something I can look back to. I wish you happiness, love, and luck in your life. You deserve so much. The sweetest human being I know, someone who actually listens to me, and cares about me. You make me feel less lonely. Thank you. Love you

To: Harry Styles

Hi Harry, I am a big fan of your music, it helped me a lot when I was in a dark place. I know you've heard that before, but it's true. When my hometown was in lockdown, I was pretty lonely. I still went to work, but that was it. No cinema, no restaurants, no going out, no visitors. All I did was work, eat, and sleep. Then I fell and broke a bone in my back. This meant no more work. Instead, I had to stay home on bed rest. I was pretty lonely in my bed alone, so I listened to your music and watched a lot of movies. I don't know if it was the loneliness or the medication, but I had conversations in my head with you. I know it sounds awkward, but you talked back. We talked about everything in life. We liked and loved the same things. It was as if we knew each other for years. I told you everything that happened in my life, and you told me how difficult it can be to be famous. You were lonely too. We loved the same food and colors, and we both took long showers. We have 36 things we like and love. Crazy huh? I've been stuck inside for six months now, and next week I go back to work for a couple of hours. I think of you every day, and I really want to meet you someday. Unfortunately, that probably won't happen. So maybe you'll read this someday and you will search for me. But for now, I will talk to you in my head. I wish you all the love and happiness in the world. You have a special place in my heart forever.

To: The Moon And The Stars

You glow so bright for everyone, and it makes me happy. Thank you for being here every night when I have my deepest thoughts. Thank you for being there when I ran away, just to look at you for hours on end before the sun came up. I know you'll always be there for me.

To: My Parents

I always hoped that the two of you would love each other the way I love you separately.

To: William

I never met you. I remember the morning your father came to me and the rest of the class and told us you had committed suicide. Your father looked like he had been ripped apart, and I don't think he will be able to put himself back together. I still don't know much about you. I'm sorry you were suffering so far from home with a life people would think could make anyone happy.

To: That One Person

For just over half a year, I have been falling deeply in love with you. I never thought I would, but when I rejected you, I realized it was because of what other people thought of me. I was scared that they would see me differently, just as I always have. I have always worried about what people thought of me instead of doing what is right for me. But I'm sick of it now. I'm sick of putting other people before myself, and I don't care anymore. I am deeply in love with you, and there is nothing that anyone can do about it.

To: Mason

"U bring me 2 climax without sex And u do it all with regal grace
U r my heart in Human Form" -Tupac

To: Maggie

You are my one true love. Even though it's not romantic, it doesn't make it any less true. You are the reason I laugh, and the reason I cry, and the reason I decide to stay another day. You make me love the summer, and reading, and wet pavement, and bike rides. You make me love life. I hope I make you happy and bring light into your life because you sure do all of that for me. I love you.

To: A Friend I Lost A Long Time Ago

Hi, it's been awhile. You've been gone for some time now and I know that, but I wish it wasn't true. I wish I could pick up my phone and give you a call, but I can't. I wish I could see you one more time, but I can't. So I'll write you this letter instead. I miss you. A lot. And I know they say that it gets easier, and in some ways it has, but in most ways, it hasn't. It was quiet for awhile after you left. No one laughed, no one smiled, no one felt. Things just kind of stopped. And then one day they moved again. Everyone slowly started to forget the pain. But it lingered around me, I think it knew that I wasn't gonna let it go anytime soon. So the pain clung, and I let it. I let it fester and infect me until I was lost in a sense. It was hard knowing that you were no longer someone I could count on. Knowing that a part of me had died along with you. You brought joy into my days and light into my life. When you left I thought that you took that joy and light with you. But you didn't. You left it in this world. You left a piece of yourself here for me to go back to when I'm missing you a little too much. There are so many things I could change, but that's not how it works. And I've accepted that now. Accepted that you are gone and there is nothing I can do about it. Every now and then your name comes up in conversation and I smile. Of course with that smile comes memories and with the memories comes silence. And finally, with the silence, I think about what would happen if I could see you one last time and what I would say. There are so many things I wish I could tell you, and it hurts to know that I will never get to share these things with you. I just wish I could give you a hug and thank you for everything you gave me.

To: Everyone Reading This

I'm sure we've all heard the words "Work for your goals" or "Achieve your dreams." As a kid, all of those sayings and whatnot really do sound convincing. But the older I get, and the closer I get to the real world, I realize that all of them are lies. You may have a goal, but if you think about it, there are hundreds of thousands of people who have that same dream. It's only a matter of who wants it more. I'm not saying you can't be whatever you want to be, but that you won't get it handed to you. You get what you earn. If you don't work for what you want, it won't be yours. That's how life is, and that's how it always will be. The more you work, the more you gain. So get up and go after what you desire.

To: My Brothers

Hi, I love you guys. Things are rough at home, I know. I'm sorry I'm not there enough. I hope you don't feel like I've abandoned you. You guys are both going through milestones; kindergarten and middle school. I will try to be there for both of you more. Things are probably rough with mom and your dad. I care about you both so much. You'll understand one day why I couldn't be around them anymore. No matter what, I'll always have your guys' backs. Be good, and please take care of each other.

To: Mom

I wish you could have been there more. I wish you hugged me a little more. I wish you were the parent every other kid had when we went on field trips. I wish you were the mom to tell me how to shave, what to do when a boy breaks my heart, or how to love myself. But you weren't her. Instead, you showed me how to abandon your children and play the victim in every situation. So thank you, mom, for nothing.

To: My Lost Loves

Love is a four-letter word that has carried so much meaning since the beginning of time. From cheesy middle school crushes to old spouses taking care of each other, love seems to be everywhere. Love is the feeling a mother has when she sees her child being born or the kind of love a father feels walking his daughter down the aisle. That is the familiar love that almost every family strives to have. Love also comes in the form of meeting the person you want to spend the rest of your life with. That type of love makes you see your partner as flawless, and it makes you think of them first thing in the morning when you wake up. But I wish I had some sort of love. My parents, who are immigrants, never could truly show me love or affection. I long for that type of motherly love. Silently I await the moment I can feel some sort of love.

To: My Absent Father

I graduated. I graduated with honors an entire year early with a double minor, but you wouldn't know. I broke up with my boyfriend after four years, but you would not know. I studied abroad, but you would not know. I'm going to teach English in Spain next year, but you would not know. You wouldn't know because you stopped being a dad. I tried, again and again, to reach out to you, but I never got a response. Not on Father's Day, Christmas, or your birthday. Nothing. They say you make time for the ones you love, so I guess I know where I stand. They say the phone works both ways, but that shouldn't apply to your child. Maybe one day, you will finally realize what you have lost. As for me, I have already mourned the loss of my father.

To: 42

I know it's been a while, even if sometimes it doesn't feel like it. I've taken a lot of breaths and celebrated a lot of birthdays without you. Already lost count. I think I can't stand another day without you, but there I am, and years have passed. I wear your old clothing, hoping to feel closer to you. But in some way, you feel even further away. I always thought the warm fabric would feel like your skin or smell just like you did. Then the sun disappears, and the only thing I can scent is myself. I know if I had the chance, I'd hug my arms around you and never let go as my life depended on it, but I can't. And what hurts the most is the fact that I'll keep on missing you forever. No ending, infinity. Like two parallel lines in space hopelessly wanting to meet, except we've already met, but for the last time, ever. That's the worst kind of pain. The one that never disappears. Because the thing you want most in the whole universe is the thing you can never get.

To: My Ex-Best Friend

I forgive you. I'm finally getting to be okay. And we were young, and you were dumb, but you never apologized, and that hurt. It hurt seeing you every day for the next three years happy, so happy when I was so sad. I saw you, but you stopped seeing me, and that hurt too. And I don't cry about you in the shower anymore. I don't lay awake at night staring at my ceiling and wondering why I wasn't enough for you. I don't even miss you anymore. So now, I forgive you with a mangled sense of self, cracked and shattered pride, but with a shine of hope for my future. Even a future that doesn't include you. I forgive you.

To: Isabel

Hi! I know you aren't probably reading this, but that's ok. I just wanted to tell you something that maybe I won't have the strength or courage to tell you in later years. You mean so much to me. I know I'm probably just that friend from camp or that stupid girl who keeps messing around with you, but I don't think you truly know how much you mean to me. I wrote to you once, trying to put in perfect details about how you've affected my life for the better, but of course, I've never been good with words, but you have. It is one of the things I admire about you. The truth is, I cannot tell you how much you mean to me because that would mean I would have to tell you that I like you. For many years, I've been deep in the closet. I don't speak much about my sexuality, and there's something in my brain that makes me ashamed of who I like. Yet when I'm with you, I feel so unabashedly myself. I can talk to you for hours on end, and we can make each other cry and laugh. I know we can't be together, which is fine. You deserve the best of the best. I'm going to miss you so much if/when we drift apart. Please don't forget me. Please.

To: Everyone

I have finally discovered happiness. After going through years of feeling lost and useless, I have found myself. I have never been happier. There is a light at the end of the tunnel for anyone who is struggling. Fight one day at a time. The day may come when you have to pass this message on to someone else.

To: Myself

Even the prettiest flowers need a little rain to grow. And when that rain starts pouring, the sun will come up again and shine on you (& your life)! It is called the circle of life for a reason. Be patient. Flowers don't bloom overnight :)

To: My Younger Self

Sometimes it won't come in waves. Sometimes it will be an entire ocean all at once for a year. All of the bad things that happen to you will feel enormous, and they will feel like your whole life. They're not. Not only will you live through it, much to your surprise, but it will all fade to the background. Summers are waiting for you, filled with days stretched out on lawn chairs and belting Adele songs in the car with your best friend. Getting older still feels scary, but I have caught myself in these sun-drenched days thanking you for staying. Stay. This summer is waiting for you and so are so many other things.

To: Mum

"I am so proud of you." I have been so lucky to hear that almost thousands of times from you, but I do not think I have ever had the chance to tell you too. I am so proud of who you were, are, and will be. I am so proud of the loving family you have raised me in. You have made me proud to be your daughter. I remember crying when you told us about your childhood and crying when I saw you upset. Even when you are angry at me, you are still my biggest inspiration. My absolute role model. I do not think I have ever truly appreciated how lucky I am to have you in my life. I know I was closer with Dad when I was younger, but something about this pandemic brought us together, helped us to find similar passions. Thank you for believing in me and my future ambitions. Thank you for taking me to art galleries almost every week. Buying me little things when you notice I like them. Helping me with my homework last year when I was in tears. Teaching my brother to cook. Always calling my sister whenever you can. I doubt that you will ever see this. Now that I think about it, I should express more of this out loud. But honestly, I think I would start crying before I could even get a word out. My extreme emotions come from you. Thank you for those too. You have taught me patience, kindness, empathy, and so much more. Whenever you see a homeless person outside of Sainsbury's, you will always stop to give them money. Or, when you give out parking tickets to people if there is still time left. And when you always stop to ask people if they're ok. I remember when we gave a lift to some hitchhikers who were too tired to get to a station. In those moments I think, I want to be like you when I grow up. And I hope to God I do because you are the best person I know. I am so proud of you Mum.

To: The Readers

In case nobody told you today, I'm proud of you. Think about that. Someone out there is proud of you, whether you know it or not. You'll never know me, and I'll never know you, but I'm proud of you. So, the next time that you have doubts about yourself, think of this letter. You are wonderful, you are beautiful, you deserve happiness, and I'm proud of you, even if you may not be proud of yourself yet. Dare to dream, friend. I believe in you.

To: Kat

Honestly, you're one of the best things that has ever happened to me. We've been through a lot together—and if it wasn't for you, I'm not sure I would still be here. We've also done a lot of stupid shit together, and it's all memories now that will last us for the rest of our lives. I can't wait to make more with you. When people talk about soulmates, you're the first person that pops into my head. I could lose everyone else in my life, and it wouldn't compare to losing you. You're my best friend, and I wouldn't have it any other way. Love you.

To: Nana

You are my biggest regret. The regret I can't even say out loud due to my shame. As you lay in the bed taking your last breaths, I knew you were trying to signal me to hold your hand. I noticed your hand waving my way. But I was in so much doubt that I was losing you, I ignored your hand, holding onto the idea that I would have tomorrow or the next day to hold your hand. You passed away alone after we all left, thinking I didn't want to hold your hand. The thought of that makes me want to come up there and find you and apologize till I can no longer speak. I miss your laugh and your company. I love you dearly and miss you every day. We all do. Never miss a moment to hold your loved ones.

To: Hudson

I think you were the first person I fell in love with. I still carry around my love confession note in my bag, just in case I ever need to give it to you. You were and still are the easiest person to talk to. It's something about the way you smile, looking straight into my eyes. I remember the day everyone found out my dad had cancer. You were sitting next to me, holding my hand as everyone looked across the room, watching the tears roll down my face. They were trying to show me that they were sorry. After that day, everyone treated me as if I was about to break. That was, everyone except you. I still remember the long talks we had at lunch about how shit our lives were, and I still remember the feeling I had when you told our whole friend group that you had a girlfriend. I wanted to crawl up in a ball and cry. The one person I loved didn't love me back. When you broke up, I felt free. I still want to tell you how I feel. I think that I still love you.

To: Those Who Need To Grieve

They say things happen for a reason, but I believe the reasons aren't always fair. Sometimes we lose people we never imagined losing, but I guess that's how the cycle of life works, right? You are born, you grow, and you die. But no one teaches us how to let go of someone. No one teaches us how to grieve or deal with loss. It is damn hard because we aren't quite sure what to feel at that moment. You get all of these mixed emotions that you can't understand or control. Sometimes you want to scream and cry. Other times you wish you could trade places with them. You can also feel tired and empty. And right when you start feeling empty and alone, you start remembering good times you had with that person, and you start wishing that they never left you. You wish you could have one last hug, kiss, laugh, smile, or just even a last glance. Letting go without saying goodbye is not easy because we don't get to tell that person how much we love them. But, when you truly adore that person with your entire heart, you know they will always be there with you, despite them not being physically next to you. The person might not be right next to you, but don't let them die in your heart. The second you forget them, they truly die. If you need to cry, do it, but don't give up on yourself. Live every day until you can meet them again.

To: A

I still love you. I don't think I'll ever stop. It comes in waves. One minute, I think I'm over you, and I've moved on. The next, I'm sitting up in my bed waiting for you to reply like old times. I know you don't feel the same way because you've made it incredibly clear. But some part of me hopes that you'll reconsider. That part eats me up. It controls me like a puppet, bending me backward and upside down just for you and your attention. I'll do anything for it, and I hate that. I'm ruining things left and right because that evil little part of me won't keep its mouth shut. I'm not sure how I should feel anymore because I'm not sure how to feel.

To: My Sister

I know you are gone. I know you are gone, but sometimes I wander into your bedroom and expect to find you lying asleep. Sometimes, when I can't sleep, I think about what animal you would be if reincarnation were real. Whenever I asked for your favorite animal, you would say unicorn. I hope they're real, even if they're not. You made me want to believe in magic, fairies, elves, Santa, and unicorns. Please, come back. All the magic is gone.

To: Me

I know things are getting hard again, and everything around you feels broken, but remember you got through this once, and you can do it again.

To: Adam

I absolutely love you. I think I might be a lesbian though.

To: My First Bully

At twenty years old, I find it hard to relate to others when they discuss the torment their peers put them through growing up. Movies depicting high school bullies go straight over my head. I was never shunned from an elementary birthday party or called ugly in science class. School became my haven from you. I think even if a classmate had made fun of me, it wouldn't have affected me in the slightest. You had prepared me all too well for bullies. Not in the typical, loving, or supporting way. You made me numbly used to holding back hot tears to seem unaffected, internalizing every small comment made about my body, and constantly feeling like I was in some way an imposter. The thing about childhood bullies is that you both grow up and move on. You forget they exist and laugh about it years later to your children. I will never get the chance to get away from you because a sick part of me still would die for you at any moment.

To: Dakota

Hey, I know we haven't talked since I moved across the country, and we both have new lives now. But the past four years I spent with you were life-changing. I wouldn't change it for the world. I miss your kiss on my forehead and standing on your boots while we danced in our kitchen the first night in our new apartment. I hope you find someone with as sweet a soul someday. I love you forever, Pineapples.

To: Him

I feel like I've written this letter a thousand times. I just don't know how to get the words right. But I guess I'll start by saying this. Out of all the things I feel unsure about in this world, you aren't one of them, and you have never been. I've spent five years trying to convince myself that we shouldn't be together. I figured one day I would stop thinking about it all. The way we fell in love by the sea, the way we held each other, and the way we both knew deep in our core that we were undeniably supposed to meet. I vividly remember the day you messaged me and told me you missed me. You said there would never be a girl that would make you feel the way I did. At the time, I felt like you were too late, and like I had waited too long. And I had met someone. I sat on my bed, a million miles away from you, sobbing, as I typed the words, " I met someone who makes me happy, and I've moved on." And I had met someone, but I'd be lying to myself if I said they made me feel the way you did. Every day of my life, I wished I would have called you and told you I felt the same way, that no one else could ever make me feel the way you did. But, it didn't happen that way. Yet, you still find ways to be present in my life somehow. I dream about you nearly every night, and I can feel us still connected somehow. I ask myself, "does he feel the same way?" I know you do. I can feel it. Every time I walk by the sea where we fell in love, I hope to see your face and wish to hear your voice one more time. I could keep lying to myself and say that I'm not in love with you anymore, but I am. And I always will be. Maybe one day I'll have the courage to tell you, but for now, I'll let life do its thing. I love you so much, and I miss you every day. I met you eight years ago, and you have consumed me ever since. Even if we never speak or see each other again, you will always be a part of me.

To: All Of You, The Lost And The Found

I`ll be brief. Do you live, or do you just exist? Answer that question. Now, if you just exist, find a reason to live. Nietzsche said, "If you know the why, you can live any how."

To: T

Hey T. I never got around to telling you this, but I got pregnant after that one night at the park when we were sixteen. You don't have a kid running around, so don't worry, I know your girlfriend might kill you. I miscarried at just under three months because of a car accident, so it didn't feel right to tell you what could have been, especially after we lost contact when you moved away. I never found out for sure, but I'm convinced we would have had a daughter. Sometimes I imagine what she would have looked like. Would she have your dark curls or my blonde mess? Would she have your blue eyes or my green? Would she be lanky like you or curvy like me? I don't know, and I never will, but it felt like a sin to keep this a secret any longer. Sorry I didn't tell you.

To: The Friend I Haven't Spoken To In Months

I miss you. I miss the conversations we had and the laughs we shared. I miss you sending me random messages for no reason at all. And asking if I want to hang out soon. It's my fault we aren't talking. It's been so long that now I wouldn't know what to say anyway. I'm sorry I complicated our friendship with unreciprocated feelings. I wish that it wasn't an issue. I should have just gotten over it, and read the signs that said you weren't interested in me. Now I'm one friend short, and I don't know how to reach out to you. I don't know if I should say anything. Maybe your life is better without me in it. You have your new girlfriend to keep you company after all, so why would there be any room for an old friend? I won't lie and say it's been easy moving past this, moving past you. But even if it is hard, I would have liked to keep you in my life somehow. Maybe it's for the best. Maybe it's easier this way. Friends lose touch all the time, right?

To: Jacob

I loved you.

To: John

I think about you a lot. I always want to see you at the youth group. I drive to school every morning to pass your school (not in a creepy way). I burn my bacon to a crisp and think of you. I cook my pancakes to golden brown perfection and think of you. I stay up late at night thinking about what it would be like to be with you. I hear London Boy and Paper Rings by Taylor Swift and think of you. I think about asking you out to homecoming but then wonder if you would ever ask me to your homecoming. I want to get to know you better because I really really like you. I know there's no way you will see this, but if you do, let me know.

To: Tyler

It's been years...but I still think about you every day. I wish I knew what true love was when we were together and that I appreciated you the way you deserved. You are the most amazing, kind, and caring person I have ever met. If we had met when we were older, I want to believe I would have grown enough to realize how perfect you are for me. Maybe one day our paths will cross again, and I can show you how much I've grown. I think a part of me will always belong to you, and that's okay. I wish you the best in life, and I still wonder if you have that guitar I got you or if you play.

To: Whoever's Out There For Me

I already know what it's going to feel like when I look at you for the first time. The colors of the world will become brighter. The birds will sing louder. I'll be happier, but I might not know it at first. It might take me a while to recognize it, but that moment of realization, I'll want to remember for the rest of eternity. When I realize that you are the one I'm falling for. That moment. I might have already met you, or I might not meet you for another 20 years. I might not know when I do. But oh boy, that moment. It's the one I'm living for.

To: Tyco

Because of you, I know what home feels like. I've learned that it is not four walls and a roof or neighbors to say hi to. Home is the instant warmth that caresses me when my arms meet yours. Home is the conversations that come easy, especially after we've been away from each other. Home is feeling your heartbeat through my entire body when I rest my head on your chest. Home is getting lost in your glacier blue eyes. You are home. And I hope I can be home for you too. I love you, you beautiful soul.

To: Harry

Thank you for making me feel the closest thing to love that I have experienced so far. I wish I could have made you feel the same. It was magic. When I looked at you, I saw someone made of gold dust and pure joy. It made my heart feel so warm and protected. Maybe one day, the universe will let us share true love and be gold dust together. But for now, all I can say is thank you. You deserve the world and more.

To: The Lady In The Sky

Here's to everything that was, everything that could've been, and everything that wasn't. I love you. I forgive you. And I let you go.

To: Food

I know now that you are not the enemy. After years of feeling guilty after eating too much or just junk, I recognize that sometimes it's okay to have a second serving of pasta or go out for ice cream. I don't risk poking holes in my throat or degrading the enamel on my teeth to have a flat stomach. I literally need you to keep living, and that dependence scares me. I have to face you, the biggest contributor to my anxiety, every day. However, I am stronger now, thanks to my incredible support system. My friends, family, and medical professionals keep me going. I will not deprive myself of you, but I also won't rely on you for my happiness. My outward appearance and how healthy I eat do not define me; my personality and treatment of others do. Ironically, by eating you, I take back the power you previously held.

To: Gabs

I wouldn't be here without you.

To: Him

It's been three years. I've waited for you for three years. There is not a single day I haven't thought about you. I wish I could be in your arms again. Feel safe. I wish we weren't 5,000 miles away. I wish she didn't hurt you. I wish you weren't afraid to tell me that you love me. I wish it didn't hurt so much. I wish I could look into your honey-colored eyes again. I wish you loved me as I love you. I wish.

To: R

I know that you'll never truly accept what you did to me. I know you'll keep hiding behind the lies you've told yourself for the last two years. I know you'll always claim that I "wanted it," or that because I'm the one who had feelings for you, that means it possibly couldn't be a sexual assault on your end. But you took everything away from me! YOU decided to not listen that night. YOU did that. Feel whatever way you want to about me, but I'll always know who you are and what you're capable of.

To: The Man Who Tried To Kill Me In A Car Accident

You thought it was the only way to fix things. You lost your family in the process as well as some friends. You had to fight for your life after what you did to me. I want to say thank you, and I forgive you. By some miracle, we're happy now. You don't know me, and I don't remember you. I do know that we're stronger than we ever thought. We're kinder. We're happier. :) I love you very much.

To: Stella

I'm new to this. Incredibly new. I don't know what I'm doing, so you need to show me the way. You are amazing, sweet, kind, funny, and so so loving. I don't want to screw this up. I don't want us to fade away. I want to love you, and I want you to love me. I know that's a lot to ask, but it's what I want, and I hope you want that too. You make me feel so happy. I couldn't explain it if I tried. You're the best girl that a girl could ask for.

To: New York City

Hey, NYC, what's up? I mean it when I say you are one of the only things bringing me up right now. Life is hard. I feel stuck and tired. I feel like no matter how much I am working, I am not getting or seeing anything in return — instead, I'm just slowly burning out. Maybe you're going to be my one big gift, and seeing you will make me finally feel like all this was worth it. Or maybe not. Maybe I have to find it all in me first. I don't know, but I do know that I want you. I do. Please come soon. I want to see you, and live in you (that sounds oddly dirty, but I promise it's not), and see all that you have to give me — all that I'm waiting for. Please come soon. I will be here waiting. :)

To: Dottie

It was the hardest thing to say goodbye to you today. Please forgive me that I couldn't hold or kiss you after you had fallen asleep. It would have been harder to let go if I held you in my arms and you didn't wake up. You were very loved, by your family and everyone who met you. I wish I was able to give you that love sooner in your life, but I'm happy you had your best life with us. And I'm happy that you said goodbye to the people who loved you right by your side, giving you kisses and head scratches. I'm going to miss you every single day. I hope you're somewhere good playing with your favorite monkey and ball that we left with you when we said goodbye one more time. I love you so much.

To: The World

GOD IS A WOMAN!!!

To: Love

We search for you all our lives. Reaching, stretching, aching. We make you a plot point in a dream of someday. We think you will appear in ribbon-tied roses with velvet petals arranged on our doorsteps. But we never stop to breathe in the wildflowers, sparklingly familiar, blooming in our own backyards. We think we will find you in rainy-day kisses, but we surge forwards as water falls around us, searching for someone. Instead, we should be searching for the wonderful something. The wonderful something in pausing, gazing up, and opening ourselves to the heavens. We are all deserving of bouquets and cliches, but sometimes in the mad rush for someone perfect, we forget who we are really looking for is you. And you are not only in fluttering hearts and fluttering touches. You are here. You are in cars with the windows down and melodies pounding, surrounding, and threading us together. Together we laugh, we are sure, and we are infinite. We are infinite in single moments that we remember with a smile as experiences of us. You are connecting us. You are protecting us. You are the light of us. And you are that much more beautiful because we never had to search for you at all.

To: Anyone Struggling With Self-Image

YOU ARE SUCH A GORGEOUS BAD BITCH! IGNORE WHAT THOSE HATERS SAY! LIVE YOUR LIFE TO THE FULLEST AS THE BADDEST BITCH THAT U ARE! KEEP UR HEAD UP.

Dear Gen Z,

Love. Four letters. One word. Love.
When you think of this one syllable, what do you imagine?
Perhaps roses on Valentine's Day and dinners on anniversaries?
Maybe something smaller? Such as hugs from behind or kisses
on the cheek?
More conceptual? Effort, trust, loyalty, communication?
Or maybe you don't believe in love. Maybe humans have
disappointed you to even that extent.
Regardless. Even still.
How is it that regardless of our differences in imaginations, it still
leads us to the understanding of the same concept? How is it
that you've had different experiences than I, and even still, you
know exactly what I'm talking about?
Because it is something that everyone tries to reach, grab, hold
close. Even those that do not believe in love still desire to be
wanted, cared for, prioritized.
It is an ingredient necessary for emotional survival.
But what even is love?
Movies portray it as a predictable journey: the two fall in love, a
single conflict or several conflicts test their relationship, and
usually, the two reconcile and make ends meet in the resolution.
Social media portrays it as large, defining moments: dates pretty
enough to capture through lenses, matching outfits stylish
enough to snap away in mirrors, surprises creative enough to
record from afar.
Books portray it as the remedy to every problem: depression,
anxiety, loneliness, insecurities.
Love from another is seen as something that makes you whole.
Dear Gen Z,
It's time to wake up.

Because it's not a predictable journey, it's more than large, defining moments, and it isn't the remedy to any problem. Don't make love your savior.

He won't give you stability. She won't solve your insecurities. They won't make nightmares go away.

And yet, and yet, and yet you still expect. You still expect love to provide so much for you. Which it can. But maybe not the things you're ready for.

Because how can you expect someone else to see your self-worth if you can't see your own? How can you expect to care for someone else if you don't know how to care for *your*self?

Let's stop expecting them to chase away rain clouds with rainbows, tears with smiles, and anger with joy. Because though it happens sometimes, that factor alone is not a constant. And if you're going to rely so much on someone else, you might as well rely on your own self first.

Dear Gen Z,

Let's open our eyes. Let's revive our minds. Let's wake up. It's time.

Let's stop believing everything we see
Stop aspiring to be everything we consume
Let's stop striving for the
"Aesthetics," the Potential, the
Unrealistically idealized future
We so badly want to have it.
Because what may seem like
A pretty poem
Full of deep meaning,
Of Instagrammable potential,
Of experienced writing,
May simply just be
A monologue

With unrelated ideas
Vague intentions
And unique line breaks.
Dear Gen Z,
Don't make love your savior.
Save yourself.

To: My Past Self

We do get there in the end. We save ourselves. We're happy now. We're living.

To: Myself

I am worth so much more than the D I got in chemistry. I am worth so much more than the D I got in chemistry. I am worth so much more than the D I got in chemistry.

To: Social Media

I think my life would be so much better if you didn't exist.

To: Her

Thank you for showing me that I was always worthy of love.
Thank you for being there on the nights where I hated myself.
Thank you for never leaving, even if it seemed like a better
option. I pray that this world gives you everything it has to offer,
and you run with it. I pray that you get out of this damn forsaken
town. Thank you for being my greatest blessing and part of my
favorite memories. If not in this lifetime, then I'll see you in the
next one, my darling.

To: The Random People I Cross On The Street

English is my third language, so I'm sorry for any mistakes.
I ask myself what the hell I'm doing on this giant floating rock at
a minimum of twice a week. I think we all do. Including you. I
know you do. I think the most common mistake is rushing too
much into that question, forgetting that the question even
exists. When you forget to ask yourself THE question regularly,
you end up thinking that your goal is to make a lot of money or
to have a lot of cars, or houses, or followers, or friends, or
lovers...and believe me, I don't think that is what you want. It is
also dangerous to ask yourself THE question too much. You end
up obsessing over it and thinking about it too much. You waste
your time asking the same dumb questions over and over.
Everything in life is about finding a balance. That is why I find
that asking yourself twice a week what the hell you are doing on
this giant floating rock is healthy. And you will probably be asking
yourself, what is my conclusion? What is my answer to THE
question? I don't think it has a correct answer, but, if I had to
guess, I would say that our purpose/goal/wish on this planet is to
find happiness. It sounds Disney, cliche, and the kind of
conclusion in romantic books that teenagers read. But I really
think it's true. Probably because I am still a teenager, who hasn't
lived that much. But all our acts of working, earning money,
spending money, buying things, loving people, jumping off that
rock into the ocean, telling that guy how many years you have
been obsessed with him, eating that giant burger, meeting that
friend for a coffee, getting drunk with your friends, watching that
movie in the cinema, and writing that letter that nobody will
read. All of it, we do to feel something. TO FEEL SOMETHING. To
be happy. You want it. I want it. They want it: HAPPINESS.

To: R

3 words. 8 letters. Say it, and I'm yours.

To: Me

I love you. I'm glad my soul chose this body for this life.

To: Nick

The last time I wrote to you, I wrote about how I was in love with you. Now we just walk past each other during school, football games, and out with friends. We pretend like we don't exist to each other. What happened?

To: Mum

I was recently reading a book based on Homer's Iliad. I can't shake from my mind how the Ancient Greeks thought of the afterlife. It seems like they knew with such surety that this life wasn't the end, that the underworld existed, and they would reunite with the dead in the fields of asphodel. I wish I were an ancient Greek because then I would know with certainty, as sure as breathing, that I would see you again. Sadly, I can't believe in anything but the terrifying thought that you're gone forever. I can't help but think that every day is another you spend rotting in the ground. I don't know when it's supposed to stop hurting, but every day of the last seven years, I have felt the same pain of your loss. Every time someone poses a question involving "parents," plural. Every time a friend's mum offers me a lift. Every day when the bus drives past your graveyard on the way to school. I really want you to come back and hug me. Please. Please, let me tell you I love you because I can't remember saying it to you. I'm sorry I didn't say goodbye. I hate that I didn't spend my days with you in the hospital. I understand why no one really told me you were dying. I was only eleven, but I wish I could have really known or understood death as I do now. So, I'm sorry I didn't go to give you one last hug. I'm sorry I was scared when I saw you frail and bald in that hospital bed. I'm sorry that I thought it wasn't my mum and that we had the wrong room because there was no way my beautiful mummy looked so terribly sad. I'm so sorry you still don't have a proper gravestone; I just don't have the money right now, and dad doesn't talk about you. I'm sorry I don't visit your mum enough. I wish you could take me to see her now because she gets confused and only speaks in Norwegian, which I am terrible at, but you could translate for me. I'm sorry I don't love dad; I don't think I ever can. I'm sorry I don't know how to help my brothers. I wish I could know you better. I feel like you're a stranger to me. I found all of your old photos and stuck them on my wall. I wish you could come and tell me the story behind each one. I often imagine what life would be like today if you had beaten cancer. I'm sure you and dad would be divorced because he kept drinking for years, and you, having beaten cancer, definitely would not have deserved some piece of a shit addict to come home to. But then again, what do I know? Maybe you could've helped him. Mum, do you think you could come back and tell me you're proud of me? Because I'm trying so hard and could do with someone who believes in me. I hate how I want to share everything with you, every accomplishment. I want to see you smile and tell me, well done, because dad never does. My brothers could do with your smile as well. You haven't missed a lot in my life. I do good at school, I keep a small group of friends, and my hair has gotten pretty curly. I'm taller and slimmer, but I don't think I look like you much, which is sad because you are beautiful. If I did, I might still at least see your smile in mine, but I can't see you anywhere. I'm a strong atheist, and I know you are gone forever. I still visit your grave and talk to you, but I know you can't hear me. So, I won't tell you or myself that we will meet again. But now, I promise to keep living life for as long as I can. I promise I will make you proud, and I promise to never forget you for as long as I live. I will tell my kids about their beautiful and smart grandmother, who fought so hard. I love you with everything I am. Xoxo.

To: Whoever Is Lost Too

I feel lost. I don't know who I am. I don't know where I'm going or what I'm doing. The only thing I know is that every time I make a move, I disappoint the ones that mean the most to me. I make plans with people and feel like staying home at the last minute. I force myself to do things that I don't want to, thinking it will grow on me, but in the end, I hate it even more. I spend my time trying to be who everyone wants me to be and less time on who I really want to be. I'm a people pleaser, and I don't know how to accept myself besides seeking validation from everyone else. I try my hardest every day when I wake up to do more things for myself because it's my life. I'm still learning, and that's okay. I may be lost, but I'd rather spend extra time and focus on trying to find myself rather than let others define me.

To: The Universe

I trust you.

To: Victoria

I lied to you today, and I feel uneasy. When you asked me who I liked, I panicked and told you it was another girl. The truth is the only girl I have eyes for is you. I know well enough that we are best friends. I know that we both are girls, but the way you make me feel is so comforting that I fell for it, the way your smile makes my heart tingle and the way your hands fit perfectly in mine. You, Victoria, are the most beautiful person I have ever met in my entire life. I don't know at what point of our friendship this feeling in my chest started getting stronger, but I do know that it is real. It is so real that it hurts. I wish I could tell you those three words in person, but I'm too scared. I love you, Victoria, and I wish you happiness.

To: My Body

I am sorry - for a lot. For hating you, hiding you, and hurting you.
I am sorry for the times I looked at you with disgust in my eyes.
The times I hated the way you looked. The way you felt.
Honestly, you don't deserve any of it. You don't deserve the
torture my mind puts you through. So, I am really really sorry.
But I also wanted to thank you - for a lot. For allowing me to play
my favorite sport. For carrying me through the day. For letting
me dance when I listen to my music. For still feeling appetite,
even though we have a history with that. Thank you for
everything. And I strongly believe that we will get through this.
Through everything. I start feeling more and more grateful every
day, but I know that it will still take lots of time to fully accept
you. But please be patient with me. I am still learning. And I am
still healing.

To: Boo

Hey, we've been together for a year and a half now, and I hope we're still together by the time this is in a book. Thank you for being there for me at my lowest of lows. I love you so much.

To: Attempted Suicide Survivors

You are not a victim for sharing your story. You are a survivor setting the world on fire with your truth. And you never know who needs your light, your warmth, and raging courage. I'm proud of you for getting through it, and I hope you are doing amazing now.

To: Carlos

It's strange how I'll always think of you. Or do I just think of the "what if" version of you? What could've been us? The what-ifs still pop up in my head. It's been five years, and I still love you. You were my first love, and I will always think of you. Maybe we're meant to be together in another lifetime. Our memories will last forever, but we couldn't.

To: My Ex

I hope she says something when you're with her that makes you think of me.

To: Josh

I used to be mad. Mad at the world and myself. Like it was all my fault. I looked at everyone as if they were the enemy. I waited for someone to notice me, my parents, my doctors, my friends. You came, and you did this thing where you saw right through me, and I've never experienced that before. You did the one thing the people who raised me couldn't. You made me feel loved. You made me feel important. You were the first person who could hug me, and make me feel safe instead of scared. The first man I could sit close to without feeling threatened, but feel at home. To my best friend, I love you Josh.

To: You

I am so proud of how far you have come, how much you have grown, how you love, how you care for others, and how you have started to care for yourself. I am so very proud of you.

To: That One Cute Guy In My Spanish Class

I had the chance to talk to you one day, but I was too nervous to make a move. We made accidental eye contact once or twice, but I don't think that was enough for either of us to be interested in sparking conversation. I've probably embarrassed myself with the way I talk or walk, or something else stupid, so chances of us talking are low. If you somehow know who this is, hey. You're really cute, and that one flannel you wore that one day was really nice. I should have asked you where you got it because now I'm in need of a flannel.

To: Joseph

We met when we were still so young. You were my first for everything. My first boyfriend, my first kiss, my first love. I cherish every moment we shared, and I look for you in all the new people I meet. I miss your laugh and the sparkle in your eye anytime you looked at me. The way your lips felt on mine was enough to make the world standstill. Absolutely nothing mattered when we were together. Do you remember the night we walked in the rain and we stopped at the old train station? You put one of your earbuds into my ear to let me listen to the songs you had been obsessing over at the time. When the sun finally started to set, you insisted on walking me home. And no matter how much I pleaded, you weren't going home until you knew I made it safely into my bed. But before we could reach my street, you pulled me underneath a street light and kissed me. Fireworks exploded all around us. Reminiscing on this night still gives me butterflies. I will never love anyone as deeply as I loved you. I want to hate you for what you did to me. I want to hate you for breaking my heart over and over and over again, but I know I am the only one to blame. It has been nine months since I finally dared to leave, and I still see your face everywhere. I miss the person you used to be. But I know that that person died a long time ago. Now you're an imposter walking around in the same skin as the boy I used to love.

To: Bear

I hope you're playing fetch with all the other dogs in heaven.
God better be feeding you good up there.

To: Anyone Who Sneezed Today

Bless you!

To: My Family

I'm transgender. There's no other way to say it. I do not feel like a girl and hate being perceived that way. I'm a boy. I'm your son, your brother, your nephew. Not your daughter, sister, or niece. You've seen me as a girl for 15 years now, but I'm not. I hadn't planned on coming out this year, but with all that's going on, I needed to tell you all. Grandpa, I'm your grandson. I want you to know who I am before you disappear. I'm still the same person though! And I still love you a lot. Aunt Maryse, I'm your nephew. Thank you for the support you gave me when I started figuring things out. Now, I know who I am! Mom, Dad, I'm your son. Stop saying it's a phase, and I'm thinking this because I'm a teen or whatever. I'm your son, not your daughter. I know it's a hard concept for you. It's foreign, and you're used to me being girly and all, but that doesn't mean you have the right to deny my identity. I trust you to support me this time. So, Dear Family, I'm not a tomboy, and I'm not confused. I am a boy. And I still love you all equally. Love, your son, brother, nephew.

To: The Right Person At The Wrong Time

You know, one day I hope we meet again. And that we get the chance to finish our story. Because it wasn't meant to end like this. So I'm going to focus on myself. And I hope that you focus on yourself too. Until we meet again, I wish nothing but the best for you.

To: Cam

I really wanted it to be you, so badly. Until I understood that you didn't want it to be me.

To: Stuart

I never told you how I truly felt. I never told you that I only ever wanted to be around you. I only joined the soccer team because of you, and the only reason I looked forward to waking up each day was because of you. Maybe I should've told you more about how much I loved and appreciated you. And maybe if I did, we wouldn't be where we are today. I still love and care about you more than I could anyone else. But it's hard to see that you just put me on the shelf like a book you enjoyed but finished too quickly. I do want to thank you, though. Thank you for shaping me into who I am today, thank you for looking out for me, thank you for always listening to me laugh, even though you laugh a lot. I'm sorry for messing up what we had.

To: Anyone Who Needs Encouragement

Get the tattoo. Take the trip. Spend the money. Buy the dress. Eat the dessert. Go on the date. Why? Because life is too short for "what-ifs?" Just do it, and dammit, have fun. Who cares what other people are going to say? Are they in control of your life? No. You are. You only live one life. So live it.

To: Myself

I wish I loved you the way you loved him.

To: B

I thought it would be weird seeing you last night. I thought right. How could my best friend become such a stranger to me? We used to stay up all night together, watching weird movies, gossiping about boys, and reliving the best night of our lives. That was only three years ago. Now, I see you, and we make small talk. You think Chemistry is hard, but you still got an A. You also stopped playing volleyball. I'm not surprised though, as I know soccer is your passion. You wear pretty skirts too because you're sick of pants. But all that is surface-level stuff. I miss my best friend! I know you miss me too, I could tell last night. We both tried to bring up deeper subjects, but the conversation died too quickly. Maybe we are just too different now. Other friendships have changed the way we view our own. It sucks that we are neighbors but never see each other. I wish we didn't go to different schools, and I mean it when I say we should hang out. I don't care if we're different because I still want to be close with you. I miss you, B, see ya soon.

To: A

I'm so happy we are friends. There is no one else I'd rather facetime 12 hours a day. Thank you for holding me accountable and making me laugh all the time. Love, M/K

To: You

Maybe you're reading this book searching for your own submission. Maybe you saw this promoted on social media and are curious about what strangers have written. Maybe this letter has caught you off-guard, yet you feel compelled to read it. Or, maybe you're searching for a sign. Well, here it is. You are loved and cared for so deeply. Even if you don't feel that way right now. There are people you are destined to meet who will love you the way you have been dreaming of your entire life. People who will demonstrate forgiveness and understanding. People who will learn your love language. People who will encourage you to become the best version of yourself. People who will support you. People who will silently admire you. People who will silently love you. Be that person. Not just for yourself but for others. And if you don't have that person, hi, it's nice to meet you :)
-Yours truly, a random soul in the universe.

Printed in Great Britain
by Amazon

67433290R00119